FEELING SAD

BY AMBER BULLIS, MLIS

BLUE OWL BOOKS

TIPS FOR CAREGIVERS

Social and emotional learning (SEL) helps children manage emotions, learn how to feel empathy, create and achieve goals, and make good decisions. Strong lessons and support in SEL will help children establish positive habits in communication, cooperation, and decision-making. By incorporating SEL in early reading, children will have the opportunity to explore their own emotions, as well as the different ways others manage theirs.

BEFORE READING

Talk to the reader about how sadness is a normal emotion.

Discuss: Does everyone feel sad sometimes? What does it feel like when you are sad? Do you think it feels the same or different for other people?

AFTER READING

Talk to the reader about ways to handle sadness.

Discuss: What makes you feel better when you are sad?
Who can you talk with when you are feeling sad?

SEL GOAL

Studies show children who learn how to identify and discuss their feelings and emotions are more likely to perform better at school, have more successful relationships, and suffer less from anxiety when they reach adulthood. Help students start a feelings journal to better identify their own emotions. Encourage them to journal a few times a week to capture how they are feeling. Emotions can be documented through words, stories, drawings, or any other way that feels right to the child.

TABLE OF CONTENTS

CHAPTER 1

WHAT IS SADNESS?

Everyone feels sad sometimes. Maybe someone teases you. It hurts your feelings. Maybe you miss someone. It is OK to feel sad.

When you are sad, you might frown or cry. You might not feel like talking. You might feel tired. Your body might feel heavy. Maybe your stomach feels sick.

Sadness can feel like **grief**. It can also feel like disappointment. Maybe you broke your favorite toy. Maybe you lost a game. Lots of things can cause sadness. But there are also lots of ways to **cope** and feel better. Sadness won't last forever.

TELL SOMEONE

It is normal to feel sad. But if you feel sad all the time for a long time, tell an adult you trust. It is important to talk about sad feelings. We can get help to start to feel happy!

CHAPTER 2

COPING WITH SADNESS

Imagine you are invited to a birthday party. On the day of the party, you get sick. You cannot go anymore.

Telling someone about your feelings of disappointment is brave. After you share your feelings, you realize you can give your friend a card or a gift when you are well. You are not sad anymore.

Every day, you eat lunch with the same friends at school. But one day, there isn't enough room at the table. Being left out can make you feel lonely and sad.

You think about your feelings. You decide to sit at a new table! Making new friends can help you feel better.

Maybe you are getting teased or bullied. This hurts. It makes you sad. You talk to trusted adults. Talking helps, and they help stop the problem. But the sad feelings are still there. Maybe you keep a **journal** to write down how you are feeling.

DID YOU KNOW?

Journaling can be a great way to **process** your **emotions**. When you feel sad, write about it. Then list what you are thankful for. Write three good things about your life. List things that make you smile.

It can be hard when someone you love is far away. Maybe your mom is in the military. You cry when you think about her. A hug from someone you love can help you feel better.

Talking about your feelings with a friend can help, too. You decide to write your mom a letter. You tell her about school and what is going on at home. You feel less sad.

Losing a pet can be very sad. In times like these, sadness can last longer. Take time to experience grief. You loved your pet. Talk about your feelings of sadness. Frame a photo of your pet. Remember the happy times you spent together. When the time is right, maybe you can get a new pet!

WHO CAN YOU TALK TO?

There are many people you can talk to if you are feeling sad:
- a family member
- a friend
- a school counselor
- a nurse or doctor

CHAPTER 3

WHEN OTHERS ARE SAD

How do you know when others are sad? Sometimes it can be hard to tell. Maybe your friend usually jokes. But today she is hiding her face. She is crying. She is sitting alone.

Try to **console** your friend. Ask her what is wrong. Listen to her. Remember a time you felt the same way. Ask if you can give her a hug. Tell her that you understand her feelings.

Maybe you do not understand your friend's feelings of sadness. But you still want your friend to be happy. Tell a funny joke! Remind her of a fun time you had together.

There are many ways to cope
with sadness. Share your feelings
with someone you trust.
Do something that makes
you feel happy. What do
you do when you feel sad?

GOALS AND TOOLS

GROW WITH GOALS

People can feel sad for many different reasons. You will feel unhappy sometimes. But there are many ways to help yourself feel better!

Goal: Start your own journal! Write about how you are feeling. No one else needs to read your notes. It can be private.

Goal: Try something new! The next time you feel sad, try a new activity. Maybe go to a quiet space and try something creative, like art. Creating something can help you feel less upset.

Goal: Talk about what makes you sad. Sharing how you feel is brave. It is sometimes hard to be honest. Talking about your feelings can feel good.

WRITING REFLECTION

Write down what it looks and feels like when you are sad.

1. Write down things that make you feel sad.

2. What does your mind and body feel like when you are sad?

3. How can you work through these feelings?

GLOSSARY

console
To comfort someone who is sad or disappointed.

cope
To deal with something effectively.

emotions
Feelings, such as happiness, anger, or sadness.

grief
A feeling of great sadness or deep distress.

journal
A diary in which one regularly writes down his or her experiences, thoughts, and feelings.

process
To gain an understanding or acceptance of something.

TO LEARN MORE

FACT SURFER

Finding more information is as easy as 1, 2, 3.

1. Go to www.factsurfer.com

2. Enter "**feelingsad**" into the search box.

3. Choose your cover to see a list of websites.

INDEX

Blue Owl Books are published by Jump!, 5357 Penn Avenue South, Minneapolis, MN 55419, www.jumplibrary.com

Copyright © 2020 Jump! International copyright reserved in all countries. No part of this book may be reproduced in any form without written permission from the publisher.

Library of Congress Cataloging-in-Publication Data is available at www.loc.gov or upon request from the publisher.

Names: Bullis, Amber, author.
Title: Feeling sad / Amber Bullis.
Description: Blue Owl books. | Minneapolis, MN: Jump!, Inc., [2020] | Series: Minding emotions
Includes index. | Audience: Ages 7–10
Identifiers: LCCN 2019021540 (print)
LCCN 2019981607 (ebook)
ISBN 9781645271604 (hardcover)
ISBN 9781645271611 (paperback)
ISBN 9781645271628 (ebook)
Subjects: LCSH: Sadness—Juvenile literature.
Sadness in children—Juvenile literature.
Classification: LCC BF575.S23 B85 2020 (print)
LCC BF575.S23 (ebook) | DDC 155.4/124—dc23
LC record available at https://lccn.loc.gov/2019021540
LC ebook record available at https://lccn.loc.gov/2019981607

Editor: Jenna Trnka
Designer: Molly Ballanger

Photo Credits: drbimages/iStock, cover; MidoSemsem/Shutterstock, 1; wnights/iStock, 3; Sue Tansirimas/Shutterstock, 4; alexkatkov/Shutterstock, 5; Fotokostic/Shutterstock, 6–7; kwanchai.c/Shutterstock, 8; Africa Studio/Shutterstock, 9, 14–15; mmg1design/iStock, 10–11; digitalskillet/iStock, 12–13; asiseeit/iStock, 16, 17, 18–19; Greatstock/Alamy, 20–21; Alexandru Logel/Shutterstock, 23.

Printed in the United States of America at Corporate Graphics in North Mankato, Minnesota.